MW00686383

Dwight D. Eisenhower

by Rebecca Pettiford

BELLWETHER MEDIA • MINNEAPOLIS, MN

Blastoff! Readers are carefully developed by literacy experts to build reading stamina and move students toward fluency by combining standards-based content with developmentally appropriate text.

Level 1 provides the most support through repetition of high-frequency words, light text, predictable sentence patterns, and strong visual support.

Level 2 offers early readers a bit more challenge through varied sentences, increased text load, and text-supportive special features.

Level 3 advances early-fluent readers toward fluency through increased text load, less reliance on photos, advancing concepts, longer sentences, and more complex special features.

★ **Blastoff! Universe**

Reading Level

Grade
K

Grades
1–3

Grade
4

This edition first published in 2023 by Bellwether Media, Inc.

No part of this publication may be reproduced in whole or in part without written permission of the publisher. For information regarding permission, write to Bellwether Media, Inc., Attention: Permissions Department, 6012 Blue Circle Drive, Minnetonka, MN 55343.

Library of Congress Cataloging-in-Publication Data

Names: Pettiford, Rebecca, author.
Title: Dwight D. Eisenhower / by Rebecca Pettiford.
Description: Minneapolis, MN : Bellwether Media, Inc., 2023. | Series: Blastoff! readers: American presidents | Includes bibliographical references and index. | Audience: Ages 5-8 | Audience: Grades 2-3 | Summary: "Relevant images match informative text in this introduction to Dwight D. Eisenhower. Intended for students in kindergarten through third grade"-- Provided by publisher.
Identifiers: LCCN 2022001066 (print) | LCCN 2022001067 (ebook) | ISBN 9781644877050 (library binding) | ISBN 9781648348716 (paperback) | ISBN 9781648347511 (ebook)
Subjects: LCSH: Eisenhower, Dwight D. (Dwight David), 1890-1969--Juvenile literature. | Presidents--United States--Biography--Juvenile literature.
Classification: LCC E836 .P48 2023 (print) | LCC E836 (ebook) | DDC 973.921092 [B]--dc23/eng/20220112
LC record available at https://lccn.loc.gov/2022001066
LC ebook record available at https://lccn.loc.gov/2022001067

Editor: Rachael Barnes   Series Designer: Jeffrey Kollock   Book Designer: Gabriel Hilger

Printed in the United States of America, North Mankato, MN.

Table of Contents

I LIKE IKE

Who Was Dwight D. Eisenhower?

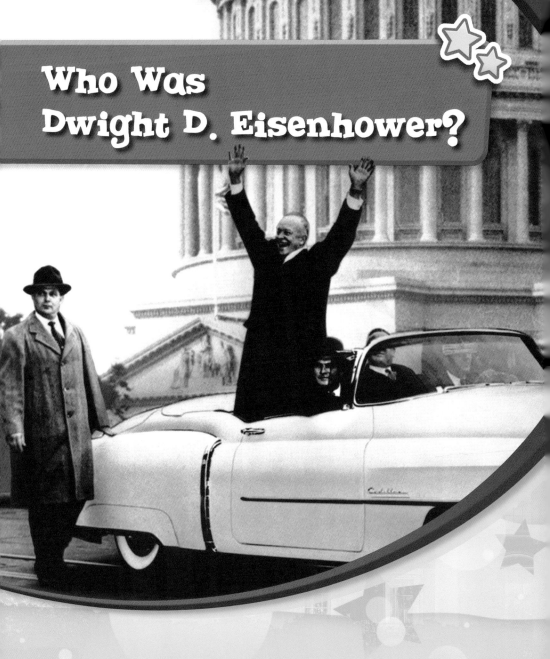

Dwight D. Eisenhower was the 34th president of the United States.

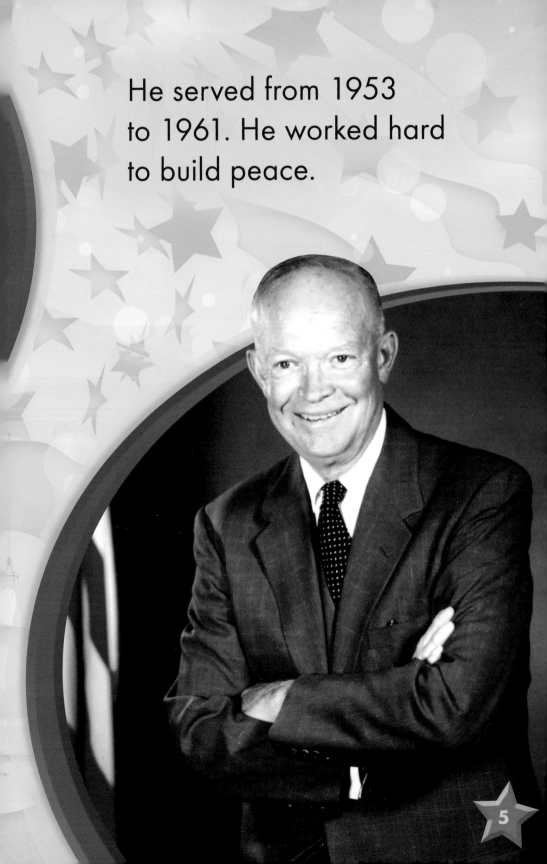

He served from 1953 to 1961. He worked hard to build peace.

Dwight's Hometown

Abilene,
Kansas

Denison,
Texas

N
W   E
S

Dwight was born in Texas
in 1890. He grew up
in Kansas.

Dwight had six brothers.
They called him Ike.
He loved sports!

Dwight playing football

Dwight wanted to be in the army. In 1911, he started school at **West Point**.

Presidential Picks

Food

beef stew

Hobby

painting

Sports

golf and football

Pets

a dog, Heidi, and a parakeet

Later, he became a general.

Dwight was a strong leader.
He led **Allied forces**
in **World War II**.
He led **D-Day**.

He was a hero! He left
the army in 1948.

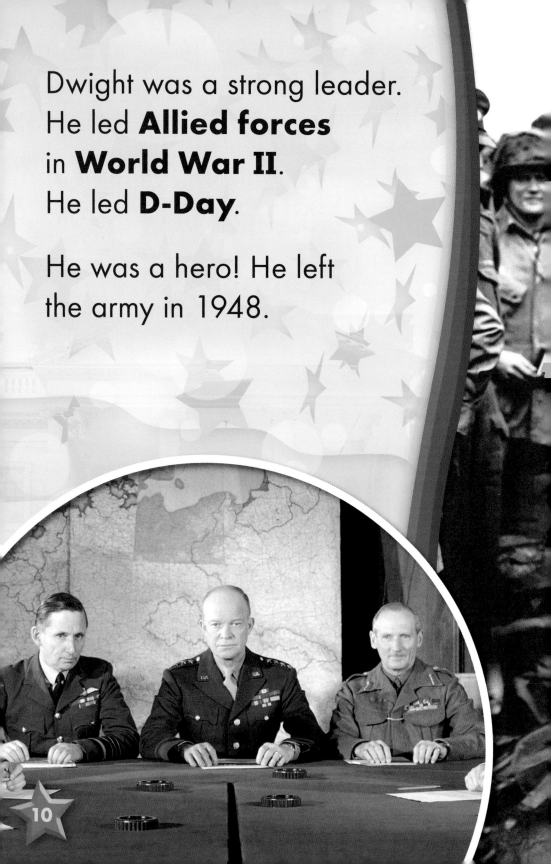

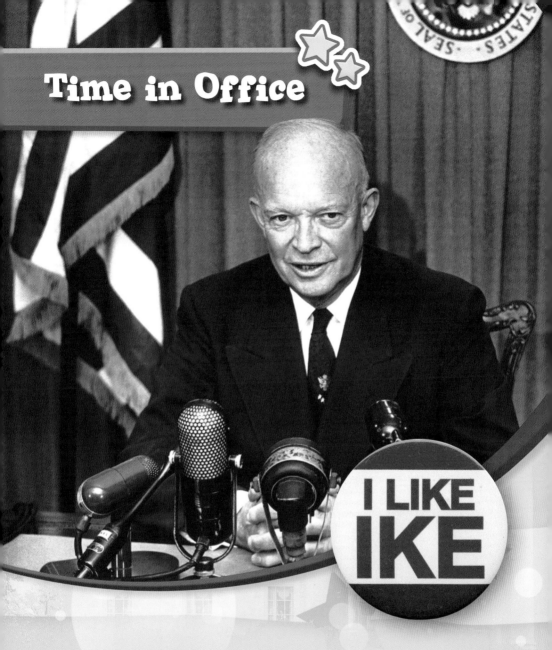

I LIKE IKE

Dwight ran for president
in 1952. His win was big.
People liked Ike!

In 1953, he helped reach a **truce** in the **Korean War**.

Presidential Profile

Place of Birth

Denison, Texas

Birthday

October 14, 1890

Schooling

U.S. Military Academy at West Point

Term

1953 to 1961

Party

Republican

Signature

Dwight D. Eisenhower

Vice President

Richard Nixon

13

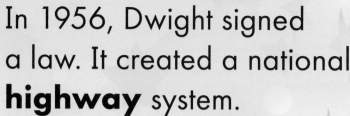

In 1956, Dwight signed
a law. It created a national
highway system.

Dwight signs the law to create
the highway system

highway

People liked the idea.
They could drive across
the country!

LITTLE ROCK

In 1957, nine Black students
integrated an all-white school.
Some people were angry.
Dwight sent troops to keep
the Black students safe.

Dwight Timeline

November 4, 1952

Dwight D. Eisenhower wins the presidency

July 27, 1953

North Korea and the U.S. agree to a truce in the Korean War

June 29, 1956

Dwight signs the Federal-Aid Highway Act

September 23, 1957

Dwight orders troops to help integrate a high school in Little Rock, Arkansas

July 29, 1958

Dwight signs a bill to create NASA

January 20, 1961

Dwight leaves office

17

In 1957, the **Soviet Union** sent the first **satellite** into space.

Dwight had to act. He formed **NASA** in 1958. The space race was on!

THE TEAM BEHIND THE SATURN
MARSHALL'S F&AE DIVISION SUPPORTING CONTRACTORS

19

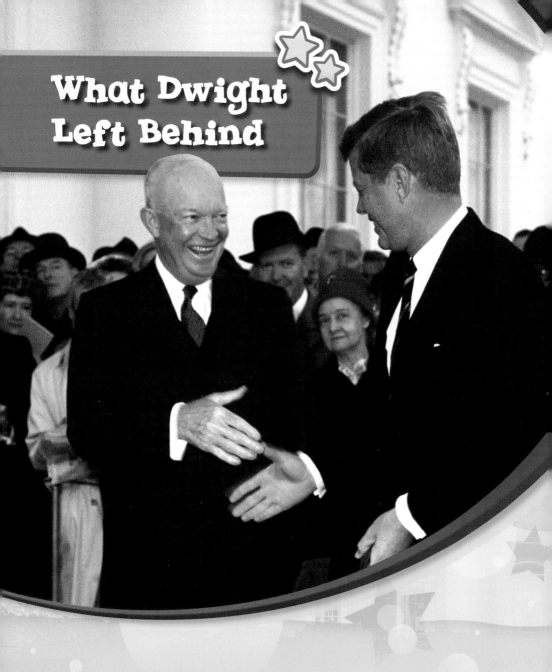

What Dwight Left Behind

Dwight left office in 1961.
He died in 1969.

As president, Dwight kept the U.S. out of war. He helped build the highways people use today!

Glossary

Allied forces—the combined forces of Great Britain, France, the Soviet Union, China, and the United States during World War II

D-Day—a large attack on June 6, 1944, that began on th shore of Normandy, France; D-Day was the turning point for the Allied forces' success in World War II.

highway—a main road that connects cities and towns

integrated—made a person or group part of a larger group; in the 1950s, integration required public places in the U.S. to serve Black and white people.

Korean War—a fight between North Korea and South Korea in East Asia; Korea is still broken into these two countries.

NASA—National Aeronautics and Space Administration; NASA is a U.S. government group responsible for space travel.

satellite—a spacecraft that moves around a planet, sun, or moon

Soviet Union—a former country in eastern Europe and western Asia that lasted from 1922 to 1991

truce—an agreement to stop fighting for a certain period of time

West Point—a U.S. military school in New York State

World War II—the war fought from 1939 to 1945 that involved many countries

To Learn More

AT THE LIBRARY

Murray, Julie. *NASA*. Minneapolis, Minn.: Abdo Kids Junior, 2020.

Pettiford, Rebecca. *Franklin D. Roosevelt*. Minneapolis, Minn.: Bellwether Media, 2023.

Rustad, Martha E.H. *The President of the United States*. North Mankato, Minn.: Pebble, 2020.

ON THE WEB

FACTSURFER

Factsurfer.com gives you a safe, fun way to find more information.

1. Go to www.factsurfer.com.

2. Enter "Dwight D. Eisenhower" into the search box and click 🔍.

3. Select your book cover to see a list of related content.

Index